ISLAMEY
and Other Favorite Russian Piano Works
Balakirev, Arensky, Rubinstein, Glinka and Others

Selected and with an Introduction by
Joseph Banowetz

DOVER PUBLICATIONS, INC.
Mineola, New York

This edition is respectfully dedicated to
Earl Wild, one of the greatest virtuosos
of the Romantic tradition in our time

Copyright

Copyright © 2000 by Dover Publications, Inc.
All rights reserved under Pan American and International Copyright Conventions.

Bibliographical Note

This Dover edition, first published in 2000, is a new compilation of works originally published separately in authoritative early editions. Joseph Banowetz's introduction was prepared specially for this edition.

We are indebted to Nikita Fitenko for his English translations of Russian footnotes, score notes, and dedications; and to Victor and Marina Ledin for research into the background and sources for these scores.

International Standard Book Number: 0-486-41160-5

Manufactured in the United States of America
Dover Publications, Inc., 31 East 2nd Street, Mineola, N.Y. 11501

CONTENTS

*In the summer of 1866, Tchaikovsky's family organized a holiday in what is now Haapsalu, Estonia, a town on the Gulf of Finland, not too distant from St. Petersburg. The first-edition cover of the *Souvenir,* published by Jurgenson, Moscow, features a stark engraving of chateau ruins—evidently a tourist attraction of the area.

INTRODUCTION

Before the early 19th century, classical music in Russia lagged far behind its counterpart in Western Europe. Most earlier music in Russia had early been dominated by Italian opera, which had been imported in the 18th century during the reign of Peter the Great, then continued by Catherine II. With this prevalent bias at court —plus Catherine's love as well for French music— foreign artists became increasingly welcomed and influential. This situation affected Russian composers as well, who were naturally encouraged to study abroad; not surprisingly, a good many went to Italy.

All this time, the rich store of both Russia's folk music and its powerful liturgical music lay relatively untapped. Moreover, folk music was considered proper only for the lower classes, although several folk-song collections were published by Vasily Trutovsky between 1776 and 1795. Interestingly, the same period saw the earliest surviving printed examples of Russian keyboard music— two sets of folk-theme variations for "clavicembalo o pianoforte" published in 1780. In those years, variations on folk melodies quickly became the most common form of piano composition.

In the transitional years from the late 18th to the early 19th century, Europe's developing spirit of Romanticism soon invaded Russia through its musical vistors, making a strong imprint on all aspects of piano performance and composition. Into this climate came influential foreign-born pianist-composers, including the German Daniel Steibelt (1765–1823), who was to become director of the French Opera in St. Petersburg; Maria Szymanowska (1789–1831), a Polish virtuoso officially honored as First Pianist to the Russian Court; and the Bavarian Adolf Henselt (1814–89), who was given the title "Teacher to the Imperial Children."

Perhaps most important among the expatriates was Irish composer-pianist John Field (1782–1837), whose compositions were to influence both Chopin and Mikhail Glinka. Settling in Russia while still a young man, Field included among his students both Glinka (1804–57) and Alexandre Dubuque (1812–98), an expatriate Frenchman. Dubuque, an unknown name today, was in fact to become the teacher of both Balakirev and of Nikolay Zverev, who in turn taught both Rachmaninoff and Scriabin. Field also taught Alexander Villoing (1804–78), whose major claims to fame were his students Anton Rubinstein (1829–94)—the greatest Russian pianist of the 19th century—and Anton's brother, Nikolay (1835-81), who was himself a great virtuoso.

By the time of Glinka's maturity, the combination of Pushkin's writings, love of country, and fury over Napoleon's invasion of the motherland had laid the groundwork for an artistic explosion steeped in nationalism—a sentiment further nurtured during the Napoleonic period (1807–12) of the reign of Tzar Alexander I, whose encouragement of foreign travel for Russian noblemen had resulted in nostalgia for the homeland and a surge of nationalistic feeling.

Now, in 1836, Glinka's opera *A Life for the Tsar* further ignited Russia's musical spirit, lighting the way for his contemporary Alexander Dargomyzhsky (1813–69), and preparing a conceptual nationalistic groundwork for the next generation of composers: Alexander Borodin (1834–87), César Cui (1835–1918), Mily Balakirev (1837–1910), Modest Moussorgsky (1839–81), and Nikolay Rimsky-Korsakov (1844–1908)—the legendary "Russian Five."

All the while, touring foreign piano virtuosos—Clara Schumann, Hummel, Thalberg, and Liszt, among the most famous—continued to make lasting imprints on Russian pianism. Following Liszt's opening concert before an audience of 3,000, in St. Petersburg on April 8, 1842, critic Vladimir Stasov wrote:

> We had never in our lives heard anything like this; we had never been in the presence of such a brilliant, passionate, demonic temperament, at one moment rushing like a whirl-wind, at another pouring forth cascades of tender beauty and grace.

It was about this time that Anton Rubinstein became Russia's leading pianist, and ultimately Liszt's only serious rival as a performer.

As contact with Europe increased through the 1830s and 40s, Russian pianism grew stronger through musical education as classes in piano instruction—although admittedly often somewhat primitive—began to be given at some schools and institutes. But it was only in 1862, when Rubinstein founded the St. Petersburg Conservatory, that Russia was firmly pointed on the road to world-class piano instruction. With the founding in 1866 of the Moscow Conservatory by Nikolay Rubinstein, Russia finally had two schools that would train the bulk of major Russian composers and performers for the next 100 years.

The increased popularity of the instrument naturally triggered allied developments. Russia saw the emergence of such piano manufacturing firms as Schöter, Tischner, Warth, and others. Russian music publishing in particular was given an international foothold by Mitrofan Belyayev (1836–1904), a wealthy timber merchant who established a publishing house in Leipzig in 1885. Belyayev eventually published over 2000 works by prominent Russian composers of the day and, as well, financially underwrote various musical societies and concert series. His role in propagating 19th- and early 20th-century Russian piano music was far-reaching.

The proliferation of visiting foreign artists, combined with opportunities for Russian performers to tour and study abroad, brought to Russia's composers an increased familiarity with Western music. Although by the early 19th century only a few of the more popular piano sonatas of Beethoven had just begun to be played in Russia, and Schubert's entire output was still unknown, this situation soon changed. Works by these composers, as well as music by such major figures as Chopin, Mendelssohn, Schumann, Liszt, and Weber, gradually made their way into the national consciousness.

From such tentative beginnings, Russian pianism—in both composition and performance—exploded during the last half of the 19th century to an unparalleled level of artistic creativity and originality. Pitted against the musical nationalism of the "Russian Five" were the dominating cosmopolitan figures of Anton Rubinstein and Tchaikovsky, followed later by those who chose a more internationally oriented road: Arensky, Glazounov, Medtner, Prokofiev, Rachmaninoff, and Scriabin.

Many of these composers were themselves virtuosos. Balakirev, Glazounov, Liapunov, Medtner, Prokofiev, Rachmaninoff, Anton Rubinstein, Scriabin, Stravinsky, and even Tchaikovsky were striking interpreters of their own works. Towering over them were the pianistic influences of both Chopin and Liszt and, to a lesser extent, Mendelssohn and Schumann. Balakirev's *Islamey*, dedicated to Nikolay Rubinstein, challenges and at times comes close to surpassing Liszt's technical extremes. It is only later—in Ravel's *Scarbo* and Stravinsky's own piano transcription of music from *Petrouchka*—that a comparable level of extended technical difficulty is reached.

In most Russian compositions of this era, sensuousness of texture and effectiveness of pianistic layout became primary elements. Difficult as a work may initially have been to read and "get in the fingers," technical difficulties ultimately seemed to fit the hand

and, above all, to sound well on the keyboard. This is particularly true of the virtuoso-composers; only Mussorgsky—himself an accomplished performer—appeared at times to write "against" the piano, not out of ignorance but for special effect.

Like Chopin and Liszt before them, the Russians of this period almost appear to regard the performer of their piano music as having not two hands of five fingers each but, rather—because of the music's frequently intertwining textures—one hand of ten fingers. Aided by imaginative pedaling, the performer is given possibilities for the widest range of tone color, voice leading, and subtleties of rubato and rhythmic nuance. It is only with Prokofiev and Stravinsky that the piano begins to be treated in a somewhat more percussive, non-Romantic manner.

The structure of music from this time and place is relatively traditional, although always with the variations one expects from unique personalities. The "character piece" so favored throughout 19th-century Europe is explored as well by virtually every Russian composer of the time—the generic étude, scherzo, nocturne, romance, ballade, impromptu, prélude, and the like; as well as such popular dance forms as the mazurka, waltz, and polka. Less common are programmatic titles and extra-musical plots. The art of piano transcription, so championed by Liszt, continues at this time to be alive and well.

The works in this volume sample the rich heritage of Russian piano music from the time of Glinka to the early years of Stravinsky and Prokofiev. Some names will be less familiar than others, but all are stellar examples of a rich heritage of pianistic and artistic creativity in Russia, from a milieu that quickly vanished with the catastrophic events of both the First World War and the October Revolution of 1917.

Joseph Banowetz
Dallas, Texas
February, 2000

ABOUT THE EDITOR

Joseph Banowetz has been described by Fanfare Record Review (U.S.) as "a giant among keyboard artists of our time," and by Russia's News (Moscow) as "a magnificent virtuoso." As recitalist, orchestral soloist, and recording artist of international critical acclaim, he has appeared on five continents. In addition to his recordings of concertos of Tchaikovsky, Liszt, and d'Albert, Mr. Banowetz has made world-premiere recordings of all eight of the orchestra and piano works of Anton Rubinstein. His world-premiere recording of Balakirev works received a German Music Critics' award as an Outstanding Record of the Year, and his recording of Rubinstein's Concertos Nos. 1 and 2 was given a similar citation in the United States by Fanfare. A graduate with a First Prize from the Vienna Academy for Music and Dramatic Arts, and a recipient of the Liszt Medal by the Hungarian Liszt Society, Mr. Banowetz has given lectures and masterclasses at The Juilliard School, St. Petersburg Conservatory, Royal College of Music, Beijing Central Conservatory, Shanghai Conservatory, and the Hong Kong Academy for the Performing Arts. Mr. Banowetz is a frequent guest on international piano juries, and his book *The Pianist's Guide to Pedaling* has been published in five languages. He is presently on the Artist-Faculty of the University of North Texas.

ISLAMEY
and Other Favorite
Russian Piano Works

Nocturne in D-flat major

(No. 3 from *24 Characteristic Pieces*, Op. 36 / 1894)

Anton Arensky
(1861–1906)

Elegy in G minor

(No. 16 from *24 Characteristic Pieces*, Op. 36 / 1894)

Anton Arensky

To Nikolay Rubinstein

"Islamey"
Oriental Fantasy

(1869, revised 1902)

Mily Balakirev
(1837–1910)

poco a poco più cresc. ed agitato

Allegro vivo M.M ♩ = 132

Ossia

Presto furioso M.M.: ♩ = 152

To Mlle. Catherine Botkine

Nocturne No. 3 in D minor

(1902)

Mily Balakirev

To Nadyezhda-Nikolayevna Rimsky-Korsakov

Prelude in B-flat major

(No. 21 from *24 Preludes*, Op. 17 / 1892)

Edited by Constantin von Sternberg

Felix Blumenfeld
(1863–1931)

"Moment lyrique" in E-flat minor

("Lyrical moment": Op. 27, No. 1 / 1898)

Edited by Constantin von Sternberg

Felix Blumenfeld

Andante *Molto espressivo e legato*

To the Comtesse de Mercy Argenteau, née Princesse de Chimay

"Au couvent"

("In the convent": No. 1 from *Petite Suite* / 1885)

Alexander Borodin
(1833–1887)

To Th. Jadoul

Scherzo in A-flat major

(1885)

Alexander Borodin

cresc.　　poco　　a　　poco

f

To Josef Slivinski

Prelude in A-flat major

(No. 17 from *24 Preludes*, Op. 64 / 1903)

César Cui
(1835–1918)

Edited by John Orth

To Theodor Leschetizky

Nocturne in F-sharp minor

(No. 3 from *Four Pieces*, Op. 22 / 1883)

César Cui

Allegretto scherzando un poco capriccioso.

To Mme. Annette Essipoff

Prelude in D-flat major

(No. 1 from *Three Pieces*, Op. 49 / 1894)

Alexander Glazounov
(1865–1936)

Impromptu in D-flat major

(No. 1 from *Two Impromptus*, Op. 54 / 1895)

Edited by Constantin von Sternberg

Alexander Glazounov

Allegro

To my dear wife

Prelude in C minor

(Op. 16, No. 1 / 1904)

Edited by Constantin von Sternberg

Reinhold Glière
(1875–1956)

Barcarolle in F-sharp major

(Op. 44 / 1898)

Edited by Constantin von Sternberg

Anatoly Liadov
(1855–1914)

Ped. al Fine

Petite mazurka in A minor

(1852)

Mikhail Glinka
(1804–1857)

"L'Alouette"

("The Lark": Mily Balakirev's 1864 piano transcription of Glinka's *Romance*)

Mikhail Glinka

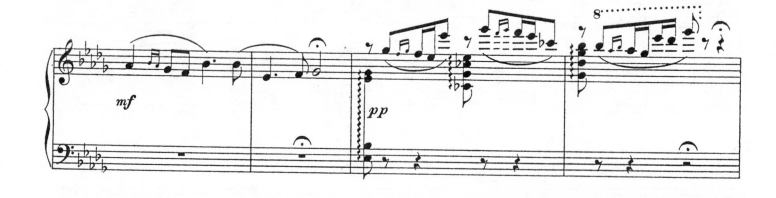

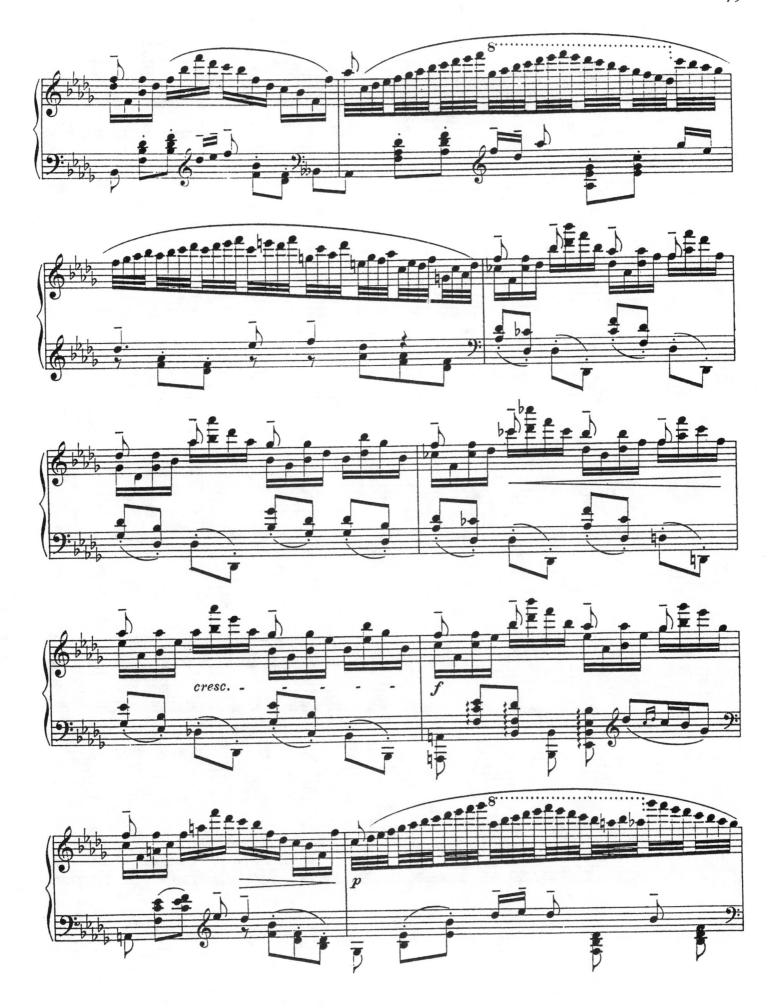

To S.V. Kreber

"Song of Autumn"

(No. 3 from *Pastels No. 1*, Op. 3 / 1894)

Alexander Gretchaninoff
(1864–1956)

To my son Michel

"A Musical Snuffbox"

Waltz-Badinage

(Op. 32 / 1893)

Anatoly Liadov
(1855-1914)

Prelude in D-flat major

Edited by Constantin von Sternberg

(Prelude No. 3 from *Etude and Three Preludes*, Op. 40 / 1897)

Anatoly Liadov

Allegro

Berceuse in F-sharp major

(No. 1 from *12 Studies*, Op. 11 / 1897–8)

Sergey Liapunov
(1859–1924)

Edited by Constantin von Sternberg

Tale in B-flat minor

(No. 1 from *Two Tales*, Op. 20 / 1909)

Nikolay Medtner
(1880–1951)

*Apply more weight on the thumb.

Tale in E minor

(No. 2 from *Four Tales*, Op. 34 / 1916–17)

"What we call ours is gone forever."
Fyodor Tyutchev

Nikolay Medtner

*It is better to keep the triplets.

To Alexander Borodin

"Intermezzo in Modo Classico"

("Intermezzo in Classical Style" / 1867)

Modest Mussorgsky
(1839–1881)

Grave pesante

To Nikolay Shemberg

Toccata

(Op. 11 / 1912)

Sergey Prokofiev
(1891–1953)

Allegro marcato.

114

To Anton Arensky

Prelude in C-sharp minor

(No. 2 from *Fantasy Pieces*, Op. 3 / 1892)

Sergey Rachmaninoff
(1873–1943)

Prelude in G minor

(No. 5 from *Ten Preludes*, Op. 23 / 1901)

Sergey Rachmaninoff

Un poco meno mosso.

poco a poco accelerando e cresc. al Tempo I

Tempo I.

To Paul Pabst

Nocturne in A minor

(No. 1 from *Salon Pieces*, Op. 10 / 1893–4)

Edited by John Orth

Sergey Rachmaninoff

NOTE. *The composer's phrasing slurs nearest the notes show the musical articulation. The longer slurs added above mark the phrases of the music. Ed.*

Miniature

(Op. 30, No. 3 / 1893)

Edited by Constantin von Sternberg

Vladimir Rebikov
(1866–1920)

To Nadyezhda-Nikolayevna Rimsky-Korsakov

Romance in A-flat major

(No. 2 from *Three Pieces*, Op. 15 / 1875–6)

Edited by Hugo Ries

Nikolay Rimsky-Korsakov
(1844–1908)

To Pyotr Adamovich Shostakovski

Scherzino in A-flat major

(No. 3 from *Four Pieces*, Op. 11 / 1876–7)

Vivo e leggieramente.

Nikolay Rimsky-Korsakov

Appassionato.

Melody in F

(No. 1 from *Two Melodies*, Op. 3 / 1852)

Anton Rubinstein
(1829–1894)

Moderato.

To Mlle. Anna de Friedebourg

"Kamennïy-ostrov"

(No. 22 from *Kamennïy-ostrov* [Rocky Island]: *24 Musical Portraits*, Op. 10 / 1853–4)

Anton Rubinstein

144

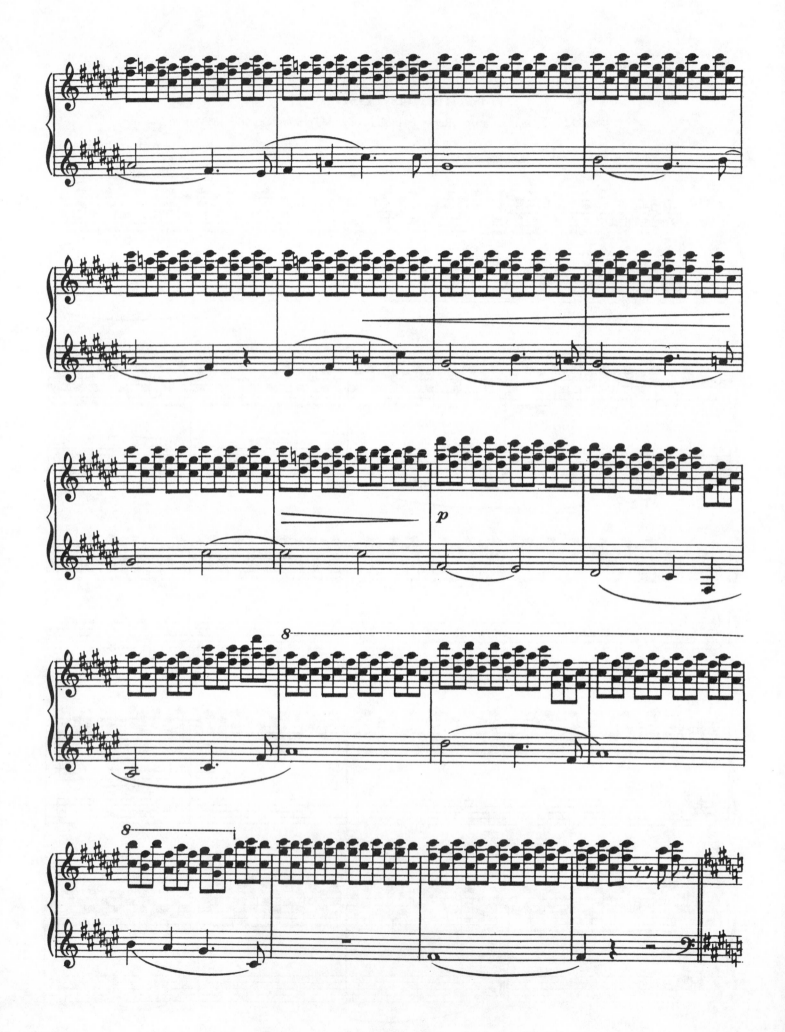

Tempo I

stringendo

Prelude in B major

(No. 2 from *Three Pieces*, Op. 2 / 1887–9)

Edited by Constantin von Sternberg

Alexander Scriabin
(1872–1915)

Etude in D-sharp minor

(No. 12 from *Twelve Etudes*, Op. 8 / 1894)

Alexander Scriabin

Nocturne in D-flat major
for Left Hand Alone

(from *Prelude and Nocturne for Left Hand Alone*, Op. 9 / 1894)

Edited by Felix White

Alexander Scriabin

To Andrey Rimsky-Korsakov

Etude

(No. 3 from *Four Etudes*, Op. 7 / 1908)

Igor Stravinsky
(1882–1971)

To Arthur Rubinstein

Piano-Rag-music
(1919)

Igor Stravinsky

*) Répétez les sol♭ de la façon la plus liée possible (legato des doigts et ped.)

To Mlle. Vera Davïdova

SOUVENIR DE HAPSAL

(Op. 2, 1867)

1. Ruines d'un château

(Chateau ruins)

Peter Ilyitch Tchaikovsky
(1840–93)

Allegro molto.

2. Scherzo

(from *Souvenir de Hapsal*)

Peter Ilyitch Tchaikovsky

3. Chant sans paroles

("Song without words" from *Souvenir de Hapsal*)

Peter Ilyitch Tchaikovsky

Allegretto grazioso e cantabile.

END OF EDITION